MATH IN OUR WORLD

WORKING WITH
NUMBERS
IN THE NEWS

By Linda Bussell

Reading consultant: Susan Nations, M.Ed.,
author/literacy coach/consultant in literacy development
Math consultant: Rhea Stewart, M.A., mathematics content specialist

WEEKLY READER®
PUBLISHING

Please visit our web site at www.garethstevens.com
For a free color catalog describing our list of high-quality books,
call 1-800-542-2595 (USA) or 1-800-387-3178 (Canada). Our fax: 1-877-542-2596

Library of Congress Cataloging-in-Publication Data
Bussell, Linda.
       Working with numbers in the news / by Linda Bussell.
           p. cm. — (Math in our world. Level 3)
       Includes bibliographical references and index.
       ISBN-10: 0-8368-9284-4 — ISBN-13: 978-0-8368-9284-0 (lib. bdg.)
       ISBN-10: 0-8368-9383-2 — ISBN-13: 978-0-8368-9383-0 (softcover)
       1. Statistics—Juvenile literature. I. Title.
    QA276.13.B87   2008
    510—dc22   2008011014

This edition first published in 2009 by
Weekly Reader® Books
An Imprint of Gareth Stevens Publishing
1 Reader's Digest Road
Pleasantville, NY 10570-7000 USA

Creative Director: Lisa Donovan
Designer: Amelia Favazza, *Studio Montage*
Copy Editor: Susan Labella
Photo Researcher: Kim Babbitt

Photo Credits: cover, title page, p. 4 (left): Brand X/Jupiter Images; p. 4 (right): courtesy of MODIS
Rapid Response Project at NASA/GSFC; pp. 5 (top left, bottom left), 13: National Park Service; p. 5
(right): © Kayte M. Deioma/Photo Edit; pp. 10–11: NOAA; 14, 16, 18, 20–21: Photodisc

Printed in the United States

1 2 3 4 5 6 7 8 9 10 09 08

Table of Contents

Words that appear in the glossary are printed in **boldface** type the first time they occur in the text.

Chapter 1

Mountain Math

Sarah reads the Sunday paper aloud. She is a reporter for her school paper. Sarah is always looking for story ideas.

She reads about national parks. The parks protect wild animals and natural areas. Anyone can visit a national park.

Sarah's mom says that she once visited Yellowstone National Park. Sarah decides to write an article about national parks.

Volcanoes

Sarah reads more. In 1872, Yellowstone became the first national park. Sequoia and Yosemite in California became national parks in 1890.

Hawaii Volcanoes became a national park in 1916. It has one of the world's most active volcanoes! Ohio's Cuyahoga Valley became a national park in 2000.

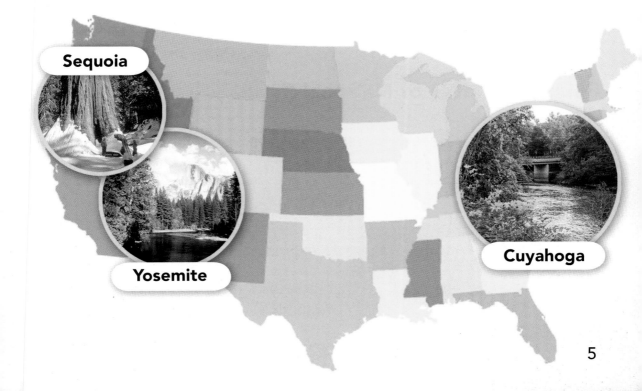

Sequoia

Yosemite

Cuyahoga

Sarah makes a **time line**. A time line is a number line with dates. Sarah will place dates in **order**. Her brother Gabe reads aloud.

Mammoth Cave National Park in Kentucky became a park in 1941. Mammoth is the world's largest known cave.

Rocky Mountain National Park was established in 1915. It is in Colorado.

Florida's Biscayne National Park became a park in 1980.

Founding Dates of National Parks

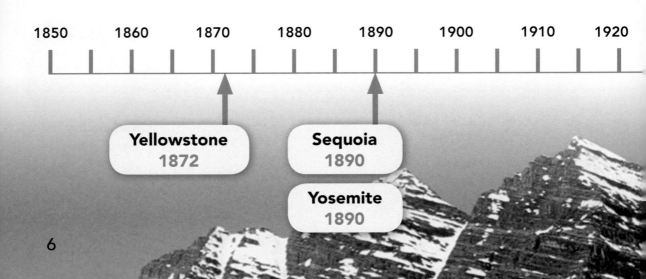

1850 1860 1870 1880 1890 1900 1910 1920

Yellowstone 1872

Sequoia 1890

Yosemite 1890

Sarah draws a line. She puts a mark for every ten years on it. She writes the years above the marks. The line runs from 1850 to 2000.

She places a five-year mark halfway between each ten-year mark.

Sarah enters the dates on her time line. Where should she put the year 1872? It is between 1870 and 1875. Sarah makes a mark. She labels it "Yellowstone 1872."

She marks Yosemite and Sequoia on the time line. They are both at 1890.

| 1930 | 1940 | 1950 | 1960 | 1970 | 1980 | 1990 | 2000 |

Gabe says that the digits for Biscayne, Yosemite, and Sequoia are the same.

Sarah nods. Then she notices that the **place value** of the 8 and 9 digits is switched. That makes a difference in the number's value.

Biscayne became a national park in 1980, not 1890. The tens and hundreds digits are reversed. Gabe says 1980 is 90 years after 1890. He writes:

1890 + 90 = 1980

Founding Dates of National Parks

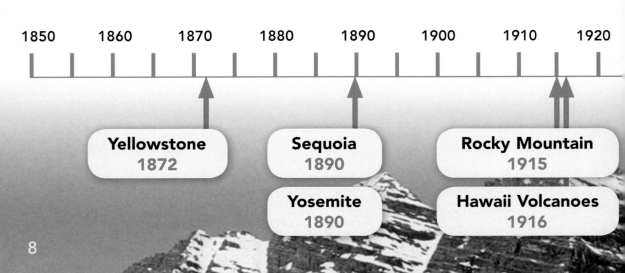

1850   1860   1870   1880   1890   1900   1910   1920

Yellowstone 1872

Sequoia 1890

Yosemite 1890

Rocky Mountain 1915

Hawaii Volcanoes 1916

Sarah finishes her time line. Gabe says Sarah's article needs pictures. He helps find them.

Sarah looks at the newspaper article again. The next section is called "Tall Peaks." It is about mountains in the parks. Sarah reads on.

The tallest mountain in North America is Mount McKinley. It is 20,320 feet tall.

Mount McKinley is in Alaska's Denali National Park.

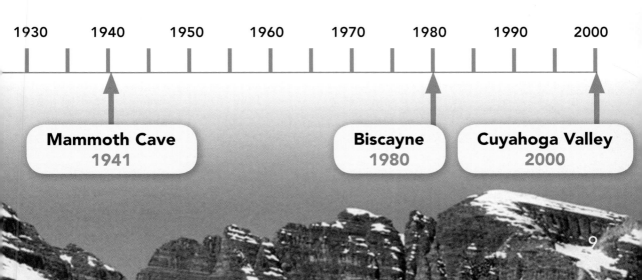

1930   1940   1950   1960   1970   1980   1990   2000

Mammoth Cave
1941

Biscayne
1980

Cuyahoga Valley
2000

Sarah reads about more tall mountains. Mauna Kea is in Hawaii Volcanoes Park. It is 13,796 feet tall. Measured from its base on the ocean floor, though, Mauna Kea is the tallest mountain on Earth!

Grand Teton is in Grand Teton National Park. It is 13,770 feet tall.

Mount Whitney is in Sequoia. It is 14,491 feet tall.

Even though it is in the warm state of Hawaii, Mauna Kea is so tall it is snow-covered!

11

Heights of Mountains
in National Parks

Mountain Name	Height
Mount McKinley	20,320 feet
Mount Whitney	14,491 feet
Mauna Kea	13,796 feet
Grand Teton	13,770 feet

Sarah wants to write about the mountains. She draws a table of the mountain heights.

Sarah orders the heights of the mountains. She starts with the ten thousands place. Mount McKinley is tallest. It has a 2 in the ten thousands place. The other mountain heights have a 1 in the ten thousands place.

Sarah compares the thousands place. Then she compares the hundreds place. She puts the mountains in order from tallest to shortest. They are Mount McKinley, Mount Whitney, Mauna Kea, and Grand Teton.

Grand Teton

Chapter 2

Tall Waterfalls

Sarah wants to do more research. She, Gabe, and their mom walk to the library. They use computers there to search the Internet. They find books about national parks.

Yosemite Falls

Sarah wants to find other things to compare in the national parks. On the National Park Service web site, Sarah reads about Yosemite National Park. She learns that Yosemite Falls is the tallest waterfall in North America. Sarah decides to write about the famous waterfalls in Yosemite.

Height of Waterfalls in Yosemite National Park

Waterfall Name	Height
Yosemite Falls	2,425 feet
Bridalveil Fall	620 feet
Nevada Fall	594 feet
Ribbon Fall	1,612 feet

Sarah wants to make a table. It will show the waterfalls in Yosemite in order by height.

"A bar graph would be easier to read," says Gabe. "It is better for comparing the heights. It will be easier to draw if we **round** the numbers."

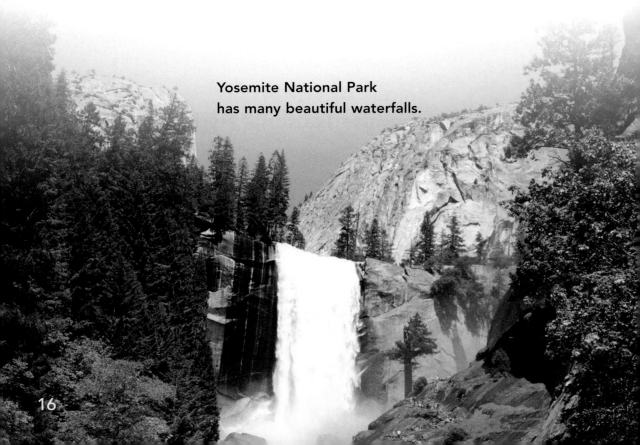

Yosemite National Park has many beautiful waterfalls.

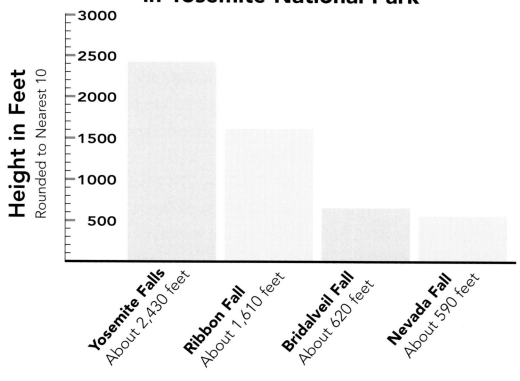

Height of Waterfalls in Yosemite National Park

Height in Feet
Rounded to Nearest 10

3000
2500
2000
1500
1000
500

Yosemite Falls About 2,430 feet

Ribbon Fall About 1,610 feet

Bridalveil Fall About 620 feet

Nevada Fall About 590 feet

Sarah discovers that if she rounds the heights to the hundreds place, it looks like Bridalveil and Nevada Falls are both 600 feet high. If she rounds to the tens place, the differences will show.

Chapter 3

Counting Creatures

Finally, Sarah and Gabe look for information about wildlife. They read that Maine's Acadia National Park has 326 kinds of birds. It has 41 kinds of mammals and 28 kinds of fish. That is 395 kinds of animals in all. They round to the nearest 100. That's about 400 different kinds.

Rocky Mountain National Park has 276 kinds of birds. It has 56 kinds of mammals and 7 kinds of fish. That is 339 kinds of animals in all. Sarah rounds to the nearest 10. That's about 340 different kinds.

Chipmunks live in Acadia and Rocky Mountain national parks.

Kinds of Animals in Acadia and Rocky Mountain National Parks

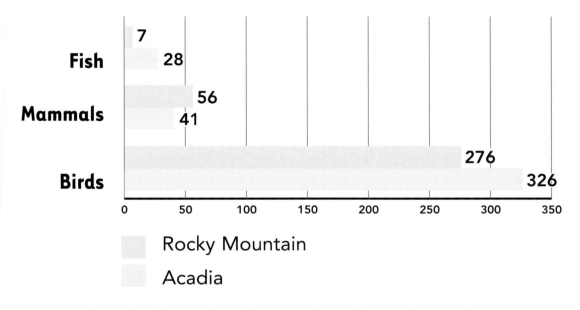

Fish: 7, 28

Mammals: 56, 41

Birds: 276, 326

0 50 100 150 200 250 300 350

Rocky Mountain
Acadia

Sarah and Gabe make a bar graph. It shows the numbers of different kinds of birds, mammals, and fish. They can use the graph to compare. It compares the numbers of animals in the two parks. Sarah makes a bar on the graph for each kind of animal in each park.

19

Chapter 4

Read All About It!

Sarah, Gabe, and their mom return home. They are excited about all they have learned. They get dinner ready. They talk about the article.

Sarah has enough information to begin writing. She says she will call her article "National Parks by the Numbers." The article has lots of numbers in it.

Yellowstone Falls is in Yellowstone National Park.

Sarah organizes her article. She orders and rounds numbers. Ordering and rounding numbers makes it easier for readers to understand the facts.

After dinner, Sarah sketches a picture of what the article will look like. She draws rectangles where the tables, graphs, and photos will go. She draws maps and pictures of animals.

Mom finds a picture of Yellowstone to use. They agree that the article will be Sarah's best yet.

What Did You Learn?

(1) Place these numbers in the correct order from largest to smallest:

1,091   2,365   1,354   3,078   12,678   12,687.

Use a separate piece of paper.

(2) Round these numbers to the nearest ten:

1,236 feet is about _____ feet.

732 feet is about _____ feet.

957 yards is about _____ yards.

Use a separate piece of paper.

Glossary

order: to arrange according to a rule

place value: the value of each digit in a number, based on the location of the digit

round: to replace a number with another number that tells about how many or how much

time line: a number line with dates

Index

About the Author

Linda Bussell has written and designed books, supplemental learning materials, educational games, and software programs for children and young adults. She lives with her family in San Diego, California.